LONGLEAT

THE FIRST MARQUESS OF BATH 1734–1796
In Parliamentary Robes
Painting by Sir Thomas Lawrence

LONGLEAT

FROM 1566 TO THE PRESENT TIME

Daphne Bath

THE LONGLEAT ESTATE

First published 1949
by The Longleat Estate

Designed and Produced by
Max Parrish & Co Ltd London

5th Edition 1967

Printed in Great Britain by
Clarke & Sherwell Ltd Northampton

LIST OF
ILLUSTRATIONS

Plates in Colour

The first Marquess of Bath . . . . *frontispiece*

Longleat House . . . . *page* 19

Son of Sir John Thynne 25

Daughter of Sir John Thynne 26

Maria Audley, first wife of Sir Thomas Thynne . . 35

Frances de Vesci, wife of the 4th Marquess of Bath . 36

Black-and-White Illustrations

Memorial to Thomas Thynne in Westminster Abbey *page* 5

Longleat from Heaven's Gate 8

Sir John Thynne 11

Longleat House 12

The Cellars 14

Lady Isabella Thynne 17

The Honourable James Thynne 18

The Hall 21

Thomas Thynne Esq. 22

The First Viscount Weymouth 23

Talleyrand's Table 28

The Dining Room 29

The Murder of Thomas Thynne 30

Bishop Ken's Library 31

Bishop Ken 33

The Second Viscountess Weymouth 38

The Roof of Longleat House 41

The Second Marquess of Bath 43

The Staircase 45

The Drawing Room 47

Six Photographs of the Thynne Family . . . . 48 & 49

The Fifth Marquess of Bath 51

The Family Tree of the Thynne Family . . . . 54 & 55

*The cover design, endpapers, and decorations on the title-page and on
pages 7, 53, 54 & 55 have been specially drawn by Leonard Huskinson.*

*The illustrations on pages 8, 12, 14, 21, 29, 41, 45 & 47 are reproduced
by the kind permission of* Country Life.

LONGLEAT

THE first impression of Longleat, looking down on it from Heaven's Gate, is gentle; gentle because its colours blend with the sky, the distant hills, and the trees. It lies lapped in a broad valley of wooded parkland, according with the landscape and the country round it.

The meaning of "Longleat" is probably to be found in the obsolete word *leat*, meaning a watercourse: there is one which runs by to the south-east.

Longleat's history begins with a priory, which stood on this site in the late thirteenth century, occupied by the Black Canons of the Order of St. Augustine and dedicated to St. Radegund. These Black Canons were not always as sombre in appearance as their name suggests, for in the description of them flamboyant robes are mentioned. "A vestment of Blew cloth of golde wrought with grenehounds [greyhounds] and Kennetts [a small species of hound] and other

7

houndes." The Monks' fishponds still exist in the "pleasure grounds", to the south-west of the house.

The Bottevilles, from whom the Thynnes are descended, first came over from Poitiers, in France, to help King John in his struggle against the Barons. They originally settled on lands in Stretton, in Shropshire, where John Botteville lived in an "inn", which in those days denoted any large house. He had a relative, another John Botteville, who was a neighbour, and so to distinguish himself from this namesake he called himself John o'th'Inne, and this appears to be the origin of the name Thynne.

The Augustinian priory of Longleat was a small and poor establishment which failed to maintain itself as a going concern, even through the Middle Ages. It was therefore dissolved during the late fifteenth century and the property became a Manor or Grange belonging to the Carthusian monks of Hinton Charterhouse. It was theirs at the Dissolution and

LONGLEAT FROM HEAVEN'S GATE

was reckoned among their properties when the Valor Ecclesiasticus was made in 1535, producing an income of about £21 a year. Sir John Thynne bought the estate in 1540. He paid £53 for it, and in the following year bought further lands in outlying parishes. The succession was therefore, Augustinians, Carthusians, Crown, Thynne.

Sir John Thynne was a favourite of the Protector, the Duke of Somerset, by whom he was knighted in the field after the battle of Pinkie, while his wounds were still bleeding. To commemorate this event he added the Scottish Lion to his arms. As the Protector, the Duke of Somerset had enormous powers of patronage, and it seems likely that he let fall much seasonable fruit into the hands of his friend. Sir John further enriched himself by marrying an heiress, Christian Gresham, the daughter of Richard Gresham, Lord Mayor of London. When Protector Somerset fell in 1549, Sir John accompanied him to prison in the Tower. After two terms of imprisonment he was dismissed with a fine of £6,000. Some years later his wealth gave rise to many rumours, including one that he had found a buried treasure, but the general belief was that he had used improper means to enrich himself. He had to appear before the Privy Council to give an account as to how he had acquired such wealth. He extricated himself from this situation with considerable skill, persuading the Council that he had acquired his wealth by his good fortune in marrying a rich wife and by "honesty and frugality". He tactfully addressed the Council, saying "My Lords, you have a good mistress, the Queen, and I had a good master, the Duke of Somerset."

Sir John Thynne had for some years been making alterations to the old Priory, and after his liberation by the Council he retired to live quietly on his lands. He had been appointed Comptroller to the Lady Elizabeth's household, by the Duke of Somerset, but in this capacity he does not appear to have given much attention to his duties. It seems possible that Queen Elizabeth bore him a grudge for his neglect of her in those days when she was virtually a prisoner, from the fact that when she came to the throne she gave him no advancement of any kind. She was friendly to him nevertheless, as appears later.

In 1567 the old house was burnt down and he started to build the present house. He finished it twelve years later.

There has been much controversy as to who was the architect of Longleat. There is no existing record to identify him, and this may be because Sir John Thynne superintended the building himself from an architect's drawings. On the other hand, there is some indirect evidence that John of Padua was the unknown artist. The Duke of Somerset had built Somerset House shortly before. It was later destroyed by fire, but from pictures it seems to have been built in the same style, and John of Padua is said to have been the architect of Somerset House. This John of Padua is a somewhat mythical person, as very few records of him have survived. It is known that a man bearing his name was summoned from Italy by Henry VIII and became "Deviser of his Majesties buildings" and that in this post he received a pension of 2s. a day, which was renewed in the reign of Edward VI.

It has been thought that John Thorpe who built Wollaton may have been the architect of Longleat because these two houses very closely resemble each other. But, in the record of his work, John Thorpe makes no mention of having built Longleat. He did go to Italy, to study Italian architecture, and it has been (rather extravagantly) suggested that on his return he called himself John of Padua, to be in the new Italian fashion! This seems, to say the least,

SIR JOHN THYNNE 1515-1580
Painting by a contemporary artist

unlikely. The problem is not soluble. We can only suppose that, as already said, Sir John supervised the building of Longleat himself, his professional architect playing so subordinate a part that his name was forgotten. It is clear from the Longleat papers that Sir John attended personally to minute details.

Sir John seems to have been a man who liked to be in the fashion. Henry VIII strongly favoured the new Italian influence in architecture, and Longleat was one of the first

LONGLEAT HOUSE

English houses to be built in a wholly Italian style. A fascinating correspondence between Sir John and his steward, John Dodd, concerning the new house has been preserved. Sir John evidently met with criticism in his venture, for John Dodd writes that "some are pleased and some are grieved". "Wild Will Darell" of Littlecote wrote a jeering address, which is supposed to be spoken by Longleat House, making mock of the builder and the new style. A contemporary copy of this is in the Muniment Room at Longleat, where it is labelled "Wild Darell's Knavery".

Sir John Thynne, writing to John Dodd, makes many enquiries as to the planting of his orchard ("I wol ye send me word how my cherry stones, abrycocks, and plum stones that I brought out of France do grow"), but usually in these papers he is urging on the building of the house. There are also letters concerning the engaging of servants for the house. "Let me have a woman to make my white [dairy], and by the advice of Mr. Berwick a man to take charge of my husbandry. Let him be both handsome and skylful, for I wol sow all my ground myself. Let me not be served in words as I have been heretofore but let the doings appear."

In support of this is the fact brought out in many of Sir John's papers which have survived, that he attended with personal care to the very smallest details concerning the building of the house. Sir John hired a number of Scottish freemasons to carry out the building and their masonic signs can still be seen cut into the walls of the house. These masons found that there was no Presbyterian Chapel for them to worship in, so Sir John allowed them to build the chapel at Horningsham, which is the earliest existing one in the country, and is still used for its original purpose. The stones in the house came from a quarry at Haslebury, near Box, of which Sir John bought one and a half acres.

While the house was building, Sir John lived at Long-bridge Deverill. A part of the wall of his house still stands there, and a superstition exists which says that, if this falls down, the family will perish.

Sir John must have been a very patient man. The foundations of the cellars were laid in 1566, and a year later all his work was destroyed by fire, but he started again nine months later.

Queen Elizabeth became very curious about these activities at Longleat. She hinted, and very broadly, that she should be shown what was going on. But Sir John, for reasons we may guess, made excuses to put her off. Sir Henry Seymour, brother of the Protector, wrote to him, "I thought it good to let you know how of late Her Majesty had speech concerning you, that you seem unwilling to

THE CELLARS

receive her this yeare at your house making excuses of sickness and other letts thereby to divert her from the country." In the end, Sir John had to face the visit, which turned out to be a success. In 1574 she rested at Longleat on her way from Bristol, where prayers were read for her safety on the hazardous journey.

Edward Hertford, son of the Protector, wrote to Sir John from the court, "Thanks be to God, Her Majesty is well returned with good health and great liking her entertainment in ye West parts, and namely [especially], at your house, which twice Sithence to myself, and the last Sonday to my Lady's grace, she greatly commended."

Sir John Thynne employed a plasterer, Charles Williams, the fame of whose skill soon spread. There is a letter from Sir William Cavendish, one of the husbands of Bess of Hardwick, in which he writes to Sir John, "Sir—I understand that you have a connynge Plaisterer at Longleat who haith in your hall and other places at your house made diverse pendants, and other pretty things. If yo business be at an ende or will be by the next sommer after this that comyth in, I wold I might have him in Darbyshire for my hall is yet unmade."

Sir John Thynne frequently had to absent himself from Longleat when he was Member of Parliament for Great Bedwyn, but while he was away he wrote numerous letters to his steward, and to his wife Christian, concerning the building and the running of his estate.* His heart seems to have been at Longleat all the time. Perhaps it still is. One feels that the builder of this house has become a part of it. He watched the walls growing for twelve years, and if ever a man expressed his love for a place in stone, he did. He died in 1580 and was succeeded by his son, John Thynne.

*Accounts he kept record the cost of the building as £8,016 13s. 8¼d.

The second Sir John was a passionate builder like his father. He completed the hall and added the oak screen and wainscoting. The hall is believed to have been butcher-blue from the evidence of some of the old colouring which has been found under existing paint.

Sir Thomas Thynne succeeded the second Sir John in 1604. He was married twice, and there are interesting contemporary portraits of his two wives. The first, Maria Audley, was painted when pregnant, as in those fruitful days this state was considered to be the zenith of womanly beauty.

Sir James Thynne, the fourth owner of Longleat, succeeded in 1640. He married Isabella Rich, the daughter of Lord Holland, a beauty of high spirit. She was one of the most conspicuous ladies of Charles I's and Queen Henrietta's Court. She inspired poets and musicians, acted in Milton's Masque of Comus, and is said to have had a taste for dancing unhampered by too many draperies. In *John Inglesant* she is described as being "dressed as an angel in loose and very inadequate attire".

The Thynnes seem to have played very little part in the Civil War, and to have stayed safely out of the way at Longleat. The only mention of the Civil War in the Longleat papers is an account of a troop of Parliament soldiers being billeted there on the night of April 30th, 1643. They plundered the stables and made off with some saddlery. Only a mile away, at Horningsham, Woodhouse Castle was razed to the ground in a fierce battle.

Charles II and Queen Catherine came to Longleat while they were at Bath, where the Queen was taking the waters in the hope that such a regimen might help her to produce the heir to the throne that she so greatly desired. In Mr. A. C. Bryant's *Charles II* there is an account of them driving to Longleat to dine. They started very late because

LADY ISABELLA THYNNE
Daughter of Henry Rich, Earl of Holland
Painting by an artist of the school of Van Dyck

the Queen kept the King waiting in her Bed-chamber while she attended Mass. The day's expedition was a rough one; there were fears of the coach overturning in the narrow country lanes, and the Queen vowed that she would never again venture out in "such a mountainous country".

THE HONOURABLE JAMES THYNNE d. 1704
A younger son of the first Viscount Weymouth
Painting by Friedrich Kerseboom

Sir James and his spirited beauty had no children. A nephew, Thomas Thynne, of Kempsford, succeeded. He was looked upon as an exceedingly rich man, and was generally known as "Tom of Ten Thousand", because he was reputed to have an income of ten thousand pounds a year, which in those days was a very great sum indeed. He lived at Longleat in magnificent style and earned fame by his tree-planting and the laying-out of a hard road to Frome.

LONGLEAT HOUSE
Painting by Jan Siberechts 1676

Tom of Ten Thousand was a friend and supporter of Monmouth (the supposedly illegitimate son of Charles II and Lucy Walter), whom he entertained sumptuously at Longleat. Dryden in *Absalom and Achitophel* (the political satire written against Monmouth, and the leader of the Protestant party, Shaftesbury) refers to Tom Thynne's lush hospitality in these lines:

> But hospitable treats did most commend
> Wise Issachar, his wealthy western friend

(Wise Issachar being Mr. Thynne).

Monmouth was a dangerous friend. He was a man always in and out of trouble, presuming on the King's tenderness towards him, and on the surprising favour both of the childless Queen and of Lady Castlemaine, with a rashness which was almost insane. Pepys describes him as "a most skittish gallant, always in action, vaulting, leaping or clambering". Nell Gwynne nicknamed him "Prince Perkin". When he secretly returned from banishment in 1679, the King, tolerant as always, allowed him to remain free on condition that he did not appear publicly at Court, and in this period of semi-obscurity he was frequently the guest of Mr. Thynne. A more astute person would have taken advantage of the King's kindliness to make powerful friends at Court, but that was never Monmouth's way. In August, 1680, the Duke made his famous "Progress through the West", starting in Wiltshire and staying some days at Longleat, and then continuing on his triumphant flower-decked way, surrounded by enthusiastic crowds, who acclaimed him as the King's rightful Protestant heir. If anyone at Court doubted that he had designs on the throne, they needed to doubt no longer. He returned by way of Longleat where he again stayed with Tom Thynne. The latter paid for these flattering attentions by being removed from his

THE HALL
With paintings by John Wootton (1668?–1765)

command of a regiment of horse in the West Wilts Militia.

These two young men fatally encouraged each other in the courses which led them to disaster. Both were to die violent deaths, Monmouth most terribly, on the scaffold, the other at the hands of murderers.

Through Monmouth's influence, Tom Thynne was promised a match with Lady Elizabeth Ogle, a young

THOMAS THYNNE ESQ.
"Tom of Ten Thousand." Murdered 1682
Painting by Sir Peter Lely

red-haired girl of great beauty who was the daughter of the 11th Earl of Northumberland, and one of the most sought-after heiresses in England. She had been brought up by her grandmother, the Dowager Countess of Northumberland, who was a scheming despotic match-maker. Through the intrigues of this stony-hearted old

THE FIRST VISCOUNT WEYMOUTH
1640-1714
Painting by Sir Peter Lely

lady, she was married at the age of thirteen to the Earl of
Ogle, heir to the Duke of Newcastle, but he died a year
later. Monmouth then used his considerable influence and
powers of persuasion to get the hand of Lady Elizabeth
for his friend, Mr. Thynne, who, in spite of his extravagant
mode of life, was still one of the wealthiest of men. His suit

was approved of, and he became betrothed to Lady Elizabeth when she was aged fifteen. Tom Thynne immediately began to make elaborate preparations at Longleat to receive this pearl of great price, splendid apartments being prepared for her and her servants, but she never came there; perhaps because the marriage had been brutally thrust upon the child by her domineering grandmother, it was never consummated. She managed to escape to Holland immediately after she had been married, and stayed with Lady Temple, the wife of the British Ambassador. Count Charles John Königsmark, who had met her in England, followed her to Holland, where he fell in love with her.

Count Königsmark was an adventurer and a man of action. He seems to have immediately decided that the only way of winning Lady Elizabeth was in the slaughter of her husband. Though Königsmark was only twenty-one years old, he had led a swashbuckling life all over Europe, and seems to have developed considerable graces at an early age. He had appeared at Court in England, where he had been admired.

Having made up his mind to murder Mr. Thynne, he set about laying his plans in a thorough and cold-blooded way. He hired his assassins (who were all foreigners): Captain Vratz, Lieutenant Stern, a soldier of fortune, and Boroski, an impoverished Pole. He came to England himself to see that his plot did not miscarry.

On Sunday, February 12th, 1682, Thomas Thynne was returning from visiting the Dowager Countess of Northumberland, in the neighbourhood of St. James's Palace. Perhaps they had been discussing his renegade wife, her grand-daughter. Monmouth is believed to have been driving with him an hour earlier. Pall Mall at that time was not a street, but a lonely road on the outskirts of

SON OF SIR JOHN THYNNE
Inscribed: · VIII · OCTOB · M · D · LXIIII · AETAT MENS · VI ·
Painting by a contemporary artist

DAUGHTER OF SIR JOHN THYNNE
Inscribed: · XV · MAII · M · D · LXXII · AETAT MENS · X ·
Painting by a contemporary artist

St. James's Park. It was a dark night, and the coach was preceded by linkmen. Tom Thynne may have been followed for some days, for his murderers had intimate knowledge of his movements. From the windows of a house opposite Lady Northumberland's, they were watching for his coach to leave St. James's Street. They mounted quickly and galloped after him, Stern reining in his horse in front of the coach, Vratz alongside shouting "Hold!" whilst he covered Mr. Thynne with his pistol. He did not shoot at him. Boroski immediately fired five bullets from a blunderbuss into Mr. Thynne's body. He did not die until next morning. Monmouth hurried to his side, remaining with "Wise Issachar, his wealthy western friend" until he died, afterwards assisting in the hunt for the murderers.

A price of £200 was put on Königsmark's head. He was seized by Gibbons, one of the Duke of Monmouth's attendants, as he was about to embark in disguise on a ship. Gibbons accused him of murder and of having been wishful of killing his master. Count Königsmark denied this.

A Grub Street ballad of the time was circulated around the town:

> But Heaven did presently find out
>   What with great care he could not do.
> 'Twas well he was the Coach gone out,
>   Or he might have been murdered too.
> For they who did this Squire kill,
>   Would fear the blood of none to spill.

There was a sensational trial. Count Königsmark was acquitted by a corrupt jury.

The other three were condemned to death, and Monmouth watched their execution in Pall Mall, close to the scene of the crime. Lieutenant Stern protested that his was a cruel and unfair fate. He said that he was about to die because of a man (Count Königsmark) to whom he had never spoken, for the sake of a lady and a dead man (the lady's husband) on neither of whom he had ever set eyes. The Pole declared that he had only obeyed orders. Both of them may well have been speaking the truth.

Captain Vratz died bravely, according to Evelyn, making no dying speech. His family wished to have his body buried in his own country, and requested that he might be embalmed. This was done by a newly discovered process. He lay for fifteen days exposed to public view, in a rich coffin lined with lead, "too magnificent", says Evelyn, "for so horrid a murderer".

TALLEYRAND'S TABLE
Upon which was signed the Treaty of Vienna
The bookcase surrounds are of Italian inlaid woodwork

THE DINING ROOM
With many of the portraits reproduced in this volume

After the trial, Königsmark could not show his face in England, and the shadow of his disgrace followed him to the Continent. He decided to wipe this out with more blood, shed in war. He entered the Venetian service and fought in Greece. He was killed at the siege of Argos, four months after the murder.

Lady Elizabeth Ogle married as her third husband Charles Seymour, 6th Duke of Somerset. She developed into a powerful political figure, having the confidence of Queen Anne, upon whom she had a very strong influence. The Tories detested her. She antagonised Dean Swift, which shows that she was brave, for this was a dangerous

BAS-RELIEF: THE MURDER OF THOMAS THYNNE
Detail from the Memorial in Westminster Abbey
Sepia drawing by L. Bennington 1850

thing to do. He turned his cynical and irascible wit upon her and circulated some scandalous verses, in which he insinuated that she had been a party to the murder of Thomas Thynne.

The poem, which was written in weak imitation of the old English style, was supposed to have been found in a grave, and was called the "Windsor Prophesy". One verse ran as follows:

> And dear England, if ought I understand,
> Beware of CARROTS from NORTHUMBERLAND.
> Carrots sown THYNN a deep root may set
> If so they be in SOMER-SET.
> Their CUNNINGS-MARK thou for I have been told,
> They assassin when young, and poison when old.

BISHOP KEN'S LIBRARY
The fourth Marchioness and Canon Jackson at left
Watercolour by Richard Doyle 1874

She never forgave the Dean for these scathing puns, and when Swift's name was put forward for the bishopric of Hereford she rushed to Queen Anne, imploring her with tears not to advance the Dean. Her plea succeeded.

There is a dramatic monument to Tom of Ten Thousand in Westminster Abbey, which depicts his murder in a fine bas-relief.

He died childless, and again a cousin, Thomas Thynne of Kempsford, succeeded in 1682, and was made Viscount Weymouth by Charles II. He lived at Longleat for thirty-two years.

This first Viscount Weymouth left a strong impression on Longleat, especially on the gardens and parklands. He laid out a Dutch garden in the new formal style which had

31

been introduced into England by William and Mary, and he was the discoverer of the Weymouth pine, which he imported into England from North America for the first time. But his highest claim to be remembered is to be found in his loyal friendship, which began at Oxford in his youth, with Thomas Ken.

After filling many and various posts, among them the chaplaincy to the Court of the Stadtholder in Holland, and to the Tangier Fleet in the Moroccan Sea, Ken eventually became Bishop of Bath and Wells, under unusual circumstances. When he was at Winchester, he refused to let Nell Gwynne have a lodging in the Close, in spite of the strongest pressure from the Court, and he won his point. Very typically, Charles II showed his disinterestedness, and discernment of character, by appointing him Bishop of Bath and Wells soon after. When the vacancy occurred, the King remembered the spirit that Ken had shown at Winchester, and said, "Where is the good little man who refused his lodging to poor Nell?" And so Dr. Ken became Bishop of Bath and Wells.

In 1688, in the reign of James II, he was committed to the Tower, with six other bishops, for refusing to publish the King's Declaration of Indulgence. The seven bishops, as everyone knows, were tried and acquitted, to the delight of popular opinion. But Ken's difficulties did not end here, as they easily might have done. He was a man of unswerving conscience. Although he was bitterly opposed to Roman Catholicism, he refused to take the oath of allegiance to William and Mary, because he had already sworn fidelity to James. For this he was deprived of his bishopric in 1691, and it was then that his Oxford friend, Lord Weymouth, offered him a home at Longleat (part of which was then in the diocese of Bath and Wells). He lived there for twenty

BISHOP KEN 1637-1711
Bishop of Bath and Wells
Painting by a contemporary artist

years, spending most of his time in the Old Library, at the
top of the house, which has ever since been known as Bishop
Ken's Library. And it was here, in Longleat, that he wrote
most of his hymns and *Divine Poems*. He led a life of
spiritual contemplation. His acute conscience never allowed
him to sink into the ease of comfort which his good friend
offered to him.

He dedicated a book of his poems to Lord Weymouth, in
lines which finely expressed his gratitude and affection.

When I, My Lord, crushed by prevailing might,
No cottage had where to direct my flight,
Kind Heaven me with a friend illustrious blest,
Who gives me shelter, affluence and rest.

The first Lord Weymouth had an only son, Henry Frederick Thynne, who died during the life of his father, aged 33. He was of a literary turn of mind, and he seems to have turned his two sisters into bluestockings, by instructing them and some of their intellectual friends in French and Italian. We obtain a glimpse of a happy period at Longleat, of an intensely cultural life flowing tranquilly within the great house, while outside, gardens and woodlands grew up into a new and more beautiful order under the first Lord Weymouth's loving care. As we would expect, we find among his books many works on husbandry and the care of woods and gardens.

He left no direct heir, and again, for the third time in succession, Longleat passed out of the direct line, this time to a great-nephew, Thomas Thynne, 2nd Viscount Weymouth. He was a child when he first succeeded in 1714, and did not go to the house until he came of age, and then only to forsake it. Indeed, his life is curious chiefly because it is so little connected with Longleat. He went to live in a small manor house in the village of Horningsham near by —an odd thing to do, for which no explanation has been found. It could be suggested that he looked with disfavour on the fantastically extravagant life of great houses, but his appearance in his pictures does not lead one to believe that he was a clever man, with advanced left-wing ideas. It seems more probable that he was very simple indeed.

He married twice. His second wife, from whom the family are descended, was Lady Louisa Carteret. She was much admired for her beautiful looks. There is a striking

Within the painting: LADY THYNN FIRST WIFE TO Sʳ THOMAS

MARIA AUDLEY
First Wife of Sir Thomas Thynne
Painting by a contemporary English artist c. 1610

FRANCES DE VESCI
Wife of the 4th Marquess of Bath.   Married 1861
Painting by G. F. Watts, R.A.

picture of her in a pink and black dress, in the Dining Room at Longleat. Sarah Jennings, Duchess of Marlborough, writes in her letters of her charm and is amazed that she should have married Lord Weymouth. Through Louisa Carteret the Essex Ring came into the family, and was at Longleat for some time.

The 2nd Lord Weymouth appears in one of the large Wootton pictures which hang in the hall. In all of these there appears an orphan boy, who was found in the woods. He became a stable boy, and was killed in a fight between two stallions.

The odd character and behaviour of Lord Weymouth gave rise to many grotesque rumours in the neighbourhood. There was a story that his stepfather, Lord Lansdowne, came to stay at Longleat, and remained for such a long time that, to encourage his departure, Lord Weymouth said that he himself was going away—which he did, and never returned.

There is another story that he had a murder on his conscience. He is said to have fought a duel in a passage at the top of the house with an unknown man, who was his wife's lover. It was believed that he killed this man, and that he buried the body at Longleat. It is possible that this terrible story is true. When central heating was put into Longleat, during the 5th Marquess's lifetime, the body of a man was found buried in the cellars. He was wearing jackboots, which crumbled away as soon as the body was exposed to the air.

The passage where the duel is said to have been fought is now known as "The Green Lady's Walk", and is said to be haunted by the spirit of Louisa Carteret.

Lord Weymouth was a Ranger of Hyde Park and St. James's Park, which is surprising, for it does not readily

THE SECOND VISCOUNTESS WEYMOUTH   d. 1736
In a dress worn by her at the Spanish Ambassador's Ball
Painting by John Vanderbank

accord with the obscure village life he chose for himself.
Everything we learn about this man is surprising, even his
death and burial. He died at the early age of forty, and was
buried in Horningsham churchyard, while his two wives
and all his ancestors were buried in the family vault at
Longbridge Deverill, with Sir John Thynne, the builder of
the house.

In every detail the 2nd Lord Weymouth's conduct towards Longleat shows a strange perverted dislike of tradition, so strange that it may have originated in some frightful tragedy.

At his death, his son was eighteen years old. He came of age in 1755. He must have found a scene of desolation at Longleat. All was disorder. The Dutch Gardens, the proud creation of the first Lord Weymouth, were overgrown with weeds. The house had been neglected for over thirty years. But it was again to be cherished, to rise like a phoenix from its ashes, and sun itself in an era of elegance.

This Lord Weymouth at once started improving the gardens, calling in the services of Lancelot Brown, nicknamed "Capability" because of his habit of optimistically telling prospective employers that the scene held "great capabilities". Cowper wrote of him:

Lo! he comes,
The Omnipotent Magician Brown appears.
He speaks; the Lawn in front becomes a Lake;
Woods vanish, hills subside and valleys rise;
And streams—as if created for his use
Pursue the tract of his directing Wand;
Now murmuring soft, now roaring in cascades
E'en as he bids. The enraptured owner smiles,
'Tis finished! and yet, finished as it seems
Still wants a mine to satisfy the cost.

Capability Brown did a great deal of work at Longleat, and he must have cost its owner a pretty penny. In addition to the landscape gardening, the Orangery and Terrace were added at this time, and are likely to have been his work. These were splendid and extravagant days.

The 3rd Viscount Weymouth, who was Lord of the Bedchamber to George III, and Master of the Horse to Queen

Charlotte, seems to have been a complete contrast to his father; he was a man who led a vigorous life of fashion and public service, and as country squire. His portrait, by Lawrence, is at the end of the big Dining Room. He has a quizzical and humorous face.

In 1789, he was created the first Marquess of Bath. His first act on receiving this promotion was to entertain George III, the Queen and the three Princesses at Longleat. The Royal party arrived on Monday, September 14th, and departed on Wednesday 16th, 1789. The news of the Royal visit was only definitely known at Longleat a week before. All arrangements had to be made quickly.

The Royal procession was to come by way of Stourton. A flag was hoisted on top of Cley Hill in the parish of Corsley (opposite which the present and 6th Marquess now lives) and a large flag flew from the top of the church spire at Horningsham.

In the Dining Room a sideboard was prepared for twelve people. There were two places laid on the side of the fire, with crimson and gold chairs for the King and Queen, and opposite them three places for the Princesses.

These were the only places laid with chairs. The other seven, probably members of the family, were expected to stand around, balancing their food on plates. The idea seems to have been the forerunner of the fork luncheon. A table was set out for the equerries in the Billiard Room, whilst the gentlemen out of livery were to eat in the office. A red carpet was laid in the passage leading to the Dining Room.

Outside Longleat, the crowd was steadily growing as the hour of arrival drew near. At half past five, the King and Queen appeared—late, as they had visited Stourton and Red Lynch on the way. When the carriage drew up in front of Longleat, the Marquess and Marchioness, and

THE ROOF OF LONGLEAT HOUSE
Showing the statues on the parapet

their three sons, Lord Weymouth, Lord George and Lord John Thynne, came down the steps to meet Their Majesties. The Marquess, dressed "in his best Windsor uniform", handed the King out of his carriage, who immediately saluted the Marchioness. The Marquess next handed out the Queen.

Lord Weymouth, also dressed in his best Windsor uniform, handed out the Princess Royal, and Lord George attended to Princess Augusta and Lord John to Princess Elizabeth, the acclamations of the people accompanying their performance.

Dinner had been ordered for half past four, but was delayed because of the Royal party's late arrival. Their Majesties are reported to have talked very freely with the

Marquess and Marchioness—they alone being heard to speak loud—the rest expressing themselves in low whispers, except when talking to the King and Queen, when nervousness probably made them raise their voices.

After dinner, "the ingenious Mr. Gunter" served coffee and tea in an adjoining room. This seems to have been a solemn ritual, rather like a traditional dance, to slow and majestic music.

Mr. Gunter carried a cup to the Marquess—the Marquess presented it to the Queen. The Marquess was then handed two more cups, which he offered to the Princesses. The ingenious Mr. Gunter then presented one to the Marchioness, and she in her turn presented it to the King.

The next day, September 15th, the people began to assemble outside the house from eight o'clock in the morning. The King and Queen with the Princesses were shown around the house, and some pleasing Royal utterances have been preserved. The King said, "I expected to have found Longleat an old, worn-out, bad house, but it is far the best I have yet seen." They were taken up on to the roof, where they promenaded upon the leads, the crowd cheering them from below. At eleven o'clock the King had intended satisfying the curiosity of the people by appearing on the steps, but a violent storm broke out. The King, remarking on the "cruelty of the weather", showed himself at the windows and the loyal crowd cheered him in the rain.

The sun started to shine again, and Lord Weymouth had the bright idea of borrowing Lord Chesterfield's open carriage for the King and Queen to drive through the crowds.

On returning they visited the Plantation, the Pheasantry, and the Dairy. The crowds dispersed, and the King said, "Everything at Longleat is very good".

THE SECOND MARQUESS OF BATH 1765-1837
In the robes of a Knight of the Garter
Painting by Henry William Pickersgill R.A.

They left on September 16th, when more crowds had
assembled to see them. The King took particular notice of
how genteelly everyone was dressed, and said that it was
the most civil and polite crowd that he ever saw, every man
looking and behaving like a gentleman.

It was estimated that a crowd of 30,000 had assembled to see "Farmer George", the Queen and the Princesses. The Royal entourage consisted of forty-five persons, with eighteen horses. Longleat had housed 125 extra persons on this occasion. It is curious to remember that George III was celebrated, and justly so, for the simplicity of his life and habits. By the standards of eighteenth-century Royalty, this *was* simplicity.

Mrs. Delaney and Fanny Burney were frequent visitors at Longleat. Mrs. Delaney was a Wiltshire woman, born at Coulston. She had a reputation for making "paper mosaiks". In the collection of snuff boxes at Longleat there is one with an intricate silhouette cut out by Mrs. Delaney's accomplished hands.

The first Marquess died in 1796. He was succeeded by his son Thomas—the 2nd Marquess—who in 1808 employed Wyatt to carry out much work at Longleat. While some of this work must be disapproved, notably his action in removing the Christopher Wren staircase, to make way for a new one designed by himself,* others of his Longleat ventures were extremely distinguished.

It was Wyatt who built the stables, which continue the style of the house so successfully that many visitors suppose them to be a part of the original structure.

It is said that to raise the necessary money to pay for these alterations and additions, the 2nd Marquess asked all his tenants to pay twenty years' rent in advance. If this is true, it shows what great wealth must have been possessed by the average tenant farmer in those days, compared with our own.

*During this operation there were discovered, under the old staircase, several coffins containing the skeletons of some of the Black Canons. These were buried in Horningsham churchyard.

THE STAIRCASE
by James Wyatt 1808

The 2nd Marquess was a silent and intensely shy man. He was also one of the first people in the country to open his house to the public, a contradiction of character which once got him into an awkward and embarrassing situation. There is a story that in order to avoid being seen by a crowd going round the house, he hopped into a cupboard in the Green Library. But by an unlucky chance, one of the more curious visitors opened the cupboard door, and disclosed the shy Marquess to the public gaze. It would be interesting to know what happened then. . .

There must have been ruthless characters amongst those early sightseers. It was discovered that, while a party was going round the house, one of them had mutilated an early Psalter by clipping out the illuminations.

The eldest son of the 2nd Marquess, Thomas, Viscount Weymouth, caused consternation by marrying Harriet Robbins, the pretty daughter of a tollkeeper. He died before his father, and left no children.

The 4th Marquess, John Alexander, was a boy of eight years when his father the 3rd Marquess died five months after his predecessor. He had a long minority, during which time he lived quietly at Longleat with his mother. Then, when he was a young man, he did the Grand Tour, in accordance with custom, and on his travels he developed a passion for Italy and everything Italian, in the way that was so frequent in the seventeenth and eighteenth centuries but grew rarer in the Gothic-minded nineteenth. In the spirit of Sir John Thynne, he engaged Italian craftsmen to work at Longleat, and thoroughly italianised the house. Sir John would probably have applauded the inlaid doors which were made for many of the rooms, and their ornate ceilings, but we in our day cannot but regret the "connynge Plaisterer", many of whose original ceilings were covered up or destroyed.

In their spare time, the busy Italians made furniture. There is a suite of original design, a table, chairs and sofa, elaborately decorated with green garlands in which black snakes are entwined.

The Chinese wallpapers, which are in most of the bedrooms, are also the taste of the renovating 4th Marquess, who set his mark at Longleat as strongly as any of his ancestors had done—so much so, that it may even be objected that he laid his exotic taste too heavily on his inheritance. There is a romantic picture of his wife by G. F. Watts. Each year she put aside two of her dresses, and thus began the collection which has continued to present times. The dress she is wearing in the picture is

THE DRAWING ROOM

Lord Weymouth in 1870, aged seven. He succeeded his father in 1896 as 5th Marquess of Bath

Lady Katherine, Lady Alice and Lady Beatrice Thynne in fashionable dress on the front steps of Longleat in 1871

Lady Alice and Lady Katherine Thynne, daughters of the 4th Marquess of Bath, in riding habit, 1871

Lady Alice Thynne, later Lady Alice Shau Lord John Thynne killed in a riding accide

Lady Alice, Lady Beatrice
and Lady Katherine in 1881
with their brothers Lord John
Thynne, Lord Weymouth
and Lord Alexander Thynne

Lord Weymouth in 1881
with Lord Alexander and
Lord John Thynne, aged 8
and 14 respectively

Lord John, Lady Bath, Lord Bath,
Lord Alexander, Lady Katherine and
Lady Beatrice in 1884

ady Katherine Thynne, later Lady Cromer
lexander Thynne killed in action in 1918

still preserved as one of the items. Another of her dresses, which is also in the collection, is particularly lovely. It was designed for her to wear at Court, when she presented her daughter-in-law, Violet. As a compliment to her, the dress was made of white brocade, patterned with violets.

During the time of the 4th Marquess, Lord Beaconsfield paid Longleat a visit. In spite of great preparations having been made to receive the august and aged invalid, including the building of a temporary lavatory in his bedroom, he does not seem to have enjoyed himself at all. He wrote a complaining letter, grumbling of the cold, and the dust in the dried-up inkwell, which he was trying to use.

During the life of the 4th Marquess, Canon Jackson, the Rector of Leigh Delamere, was a constant visitor. It was he who catalogued the Longleat papers. He did great and valuable research in the Library and Muniment Room, and it is through his labour that the history of the house can be traced so clearly. For some years he stayed at Longleat during the most of the week, and then rode back to his parish to preach his Sunday sermon.

John Alexander, the 4th Marquess, died in 1896 in Venice, and his son Thomas Henry became the 5th Marquess. He will be remembered with affection by many people today. He was a very handsome man, with the addition of perfect and natural good manners.

In the war of 1914, the house was a convalescent hospital, but in the last war the large American Hospital at Longleat was housed in its own huts built in the Park. The huts are still there. An Air Force camp sprang up there, too, and many noble trees had to be sacrificed to make way for Nissen huts. The house was not wanted for war purposes till 1940, but when the Royal School for Officers' Daughters

THE FIFTH MARQUESS OF BATH   1862-1946
Painting by Sir William Orpen R.A.

had their building in Bath requisitioned by the Admiralty, and were consequently homeless, Lord Bath volunteered to accommodate them.

He was a widower, living alone. He stayed on there, keeping a small suite of private rooms for himself, while the busy life of the school went on around him. He found it interesting. Gradually he became a part of the school, and in his room there would always be a row of plates, on which were slices of the schoolgirls' birthday cakes.

The girls wore dark-blue hooded capes, lined with crimson, and they looked very decorative and gay in the landscape, and against the grey stone background of the house. Many of these girls, at an impressionable age, will carry romantic memories of Longleat all through their lives. To move from a city, even so beautiful as Bath, into rustic surroundings; to change the shut-in life of a town for the freedom of the woods and the beauty of green parklands, must have been a happy event in many lives. When they had to learn Macaulay's poem on the Spanish Armada, when they recited in their elocution class

O'er Longleat's Towers, o'er Cranborne's Oaks,
the fiery herald flew

they were at Longleat, playing their part in the procession down the ages.

The late Lord Bath died in 1946 whilst the Royal School was still his guest at Longleat. He was buried at Longbridge Deverill, and the schoolgirls, in their blue and crimson capes, lined the steps as he left his home.

Twice in its history Longleat has not been inhabited. It was neglected in the 2nd Viscount Weymouth's time. Today it is not possible for the family to live there, although it is hoped that another generation may learn to love it as the last one did.

In the old nurseries, now quiet and empty, there are the heights of three generations of children marked against the day-nursery door. They were measured year by year as they grew from nursery to schoolroom.

The heart of a house is the human life within its walls. That is far more important than its decoration or its furnishing. At the present time there is no family life lived day by day and night by night beneath its roof. There are no children being measured against the nursery door. But the house is not divorced from life. It is being visited as a thing of beauty in a drab and dreary world.

Let us hope that Longleat will really live again, not as a museum, but as Sir John Thynne, its builder, intended it to be—a home for the family.

THE FAMILY TREE OF THE THYNNES

THE FAMILY TREE OF THE THYNNES

dating from Sir John Thynne, the Builder of Longleat, until the present generation, showing the direct line of descent.

2nd wife
Dorothy, dr. of Sir
William Wroughton, Kt.   ====   †Sir John Thynne, Kt., Buil
of Longleat. D. 1.

†Sir John Thynne, Kt. D. 1

1st wife
Mary, dr. of Lord Audley   ====   †Sir Thomas Thynne, Kt. D. c. 1

Sir James Thynne, Kt.   ====   Isabella, dr. of   Thomas Thy
D. 1670   the Earl of Holland   D. c. 1

†Thomas Thynne   ====   Elizabeth, dr. of   †Thomas (Thynne)
("Tom o' Ten Thousand")   the Earl of   Viscount Weymo
Assassinated 1682   Northumberland   D. 1

Henry Thynne. D. 1708   ====   Grace, dr. of Sir George Str
without male issue

†Thomas (Thynne)
Viscount Weymouth. B
(posthumously) 1

†Thomas (Thyn
1st Marquess
Bath, K.G. D. 17

†Thomas (Thynne) 2
Marquess of Ba
K.G. D. March 18

Thomas (Thynne)   † Henry Freder
Visct. Weymouth   (Thynne) 3rd Marqu
D. 1837 w. issue   of Bath. D. 18
‖
Harriet   † John Alexan
Robbins   (Thynne) 4th Marqu
of Bath. D. 18

Thomas Henry (Thynn
5th Marquess
Bath, K.G. D. 19

John Alexander (Thynne)   Virginia Penelope ==== †Henry Frederick (Thynne) 6t
Viscount Weymouth.   dr. of Allan Parsons.   Marquess of Bath. B. 190
Killed in action 1916   Married 1953

Silvy Cerne   Alexander George Thynne,   Christopher Jc
B. 1958   Viscount Weymouth. B. 1932   Thynne. B. 19

The descent of Longleat is shown by a dagger.

1st wife
Christian, dr. of Sir Richard Gresham, Kt., Lord Mayor of London

Joan, dr. of Sir Rowland Hayward, Kt., Lord Mayor of London

2nd wife
Catherine, dr. of Charles Lyle-Howard

Stuarta, dr. of Walter Balquanquill	*Sir Henry Frederick Thynne, 1st Bart. D. 1680* ══	*Mary, dr. of Lord Coventry*
Frances, dr. of 2nd Earl of Winchelsea (Finch)	*Henry Frederick Thynne of Old Windsor. D. 1705* ══	*Dorothy, dr. of Francis Phillips*

Thomas Thynne. D. 1710 ══ *Mary, dr. of the Earl of Jersey*

Louisa, dr. of the Earl of Granville (2nd wife)

Elizabeth, dr. of the Duke of Portland

Isabella Elizabeth, dr. of Viscount Torrington

Harriet, dr. of Lord Ashburton

Frances Isabella Catherine, dr. of Viscount de Vesci

Violet Caroline, dr. of Sir Charles Mordaunt, Bart.

Daphne, dr. of Lord Vivian Married 1927. Marriage dissolved 1953	*Kathleen*	*Emma*	*Mary*

Valentine Charles Thynne. B. 1937   *Caroline Jane. B. 1928*
‖
David Robert Somerset. Married 1950